Soil. Water. Truth.

a life, a death and a rebirth

VersAnnette Blackman

BookLeaf Publishing

India | USA | UK

Made with ❤ on the BookLeaf Publishing Platform
www.bookleafpub.in
www.bookleafpub.com

Dedication

for William Charles Weatherspoon, a.k.a "Chuckie"
1984-2017
rest on, little bro
allow big sister
to finish your sentence
one last time

Preface

My prayer is to be in the space of God, and have the space of God live and breathe through me, as I live and breathe through it.

-Oprah

I am not known to miss words. In fact, I sometimes collect too many words for my brain capacity. But I can tell stories. I love storytelling. It gives power and ample space to connect over truth. Ahhh, and the lush grandeur of the metaphor! Writing this book has taught me many lessons. The most profound is this: the power to shape a story and give it life is vital to my survival and well-being.

So here goes.

It all started with the suicide of my younger brother, William. After his funeral, I tried to keep on keeping on as if I could just move through this trauma as I had so many times before. Before I knew it, I experienced a psychotic break (aka the nervous breakdown) and was living in an alternate reality, which can also be described as a manic episode. What followed was a diagnosis of Bipolar Type 1 and a vacation in a Behavioral Health hospital. But this isn't really about being Bipolar. This book is about the kind of debilitating grief that nestles so deep in our bones that we don't know that we're actually grieving. How the mind breaks down, and the spirit is attuned to everything around you. It's about the growth that happens as a result. How imperfect the healing process is. It's about how grace is the only thing that gets you through, moment to moment, trying so hard to find a tiny slice of something to keep living for. It's about giving up, and then realizing you don't have to. It's about finally realizing that you are just a tiny human, with a tiny human brain and GOD, aka the Great Omnipotent Divine is holding you up, keeping you close, and walking alongside you.

So yeah. This book is about a lot.

But the great thing about poetry is that it can be read at any point. There is no start or finish, it just is. A poem is an infinite stream of words set to convey and expose. That's my position as the writer. May this book reach you, wherever you are. And may you see yourself reflected in these truths, knowing that deep soul healing is possible and that you can make it to the other side.

Acknowledgements

My deepest appreciation to the following individuals for nurturing the seed this book was for so many years before it was published:

Soweto, who through it all did everything short of giving me his last breath, just so I could get better and come back. I honor you fully for the warrior you are, and the way you love me without question.

Laura, who always showed up with the tools I needed most. Pens, journals, books, and wine. Your compassion and support are infinite, and I am grateful.

Delana turned 48 hours on her couch into a respite and sanctuary when I was a zombie on antidepressants and antipsychotic medications. Your friendship gave me life when I needed it most.

For Lizard, rb, Aaron, and for how the love is still strong.

Cheryl, Julia and the Csiky family for that February weekend retreat where for the first time this book made actual sense.

For every permission giver, every encourager and uplifter who crossed my path even when I was manic and depressed, grieving, angry, hallucinating and repressed - you helped me. Gratitude.

For Willow Creek Community Church, Pastor Steve Carter and the entire team of folks who endured 2018. This book idea was conceived at the Celebration of Hope in 2017, (after I spent 18 hours painting that Human Trafficking mural) where I saw the words Soil & Water at the Africa stations, then heard that these words had more to teach me.

To God be the Glory.

prayer

from sight to seed
with knees in flight
i kiss the earth.
greeting the sun
with solemn songs
that stretch the eyes to intention
to see beyond what i see
giving ears to gravity --
with feet planted firmly...
and what i hear
i keep.

an open letter to the dying house plant

i'm told that your presence breathes light
that oxygen and soil are your truth
i'm told that you need
to hear me sing in order to survive
and that gift revives my youth
i'm told that without you i cannot remember
how God grows us;
each of us
how our seeds are sown and promises are born
and we reach higher and higher
arms outstretched towards the sun
see you –
you bleed inspiration in this place
we look to you for faith
you are small miracles that shine
reminding us that with just a little water a little light
we can bloom big like cherry blossom trees
we are also reminded that if forgotten
we wilt
our shoulders droop like weeping willows
but when we are resurrected we grow
and grow
and grow

and grow
so –
please.
i ask you
just live.

to grieve, to be one with all

after any tragedy—
transpires
truth
and transformation.

witness the breath of
one who sits at the feet
of the ocean or sea
each morning to grieve.
see a moon full of itself
swallow its own shadow whole
imagine hope
carving a door
inside your favorite tree trunk
leaving just enough
space for the heart to disappear
within the roots
fear creeping up branches
to release its remnants back out to the wind
allow destiny
to trace a new name

to be etched in the skies
feel earth greet

the universe
as an estranged lover
torn between what was
and all that can no longer be
see stillness and solitude
as a moment of infinite growth
hold evolution like a grain of sand

be baptized
in saltwater
be baptized
in dirt-drenched hands
outstretched
with great grace
and servitude
to every little
living thing.

the world it softly lulls

upon waking
the world i have always witnessed
now bears witness to me.
here --
trapped inside my own pure heart
spinning on an axis of vulnerability
and gut-wrenching truth,
my mind gets tired.
my soul speaks and stands
all in one breath.
and i am here in the center of it all.
first one to reach, last one to teach.
my tears boil up inside my lungs
who really knows this pain?
who can actually speak my truth, but me?
and where is the voice i used to know,
and trust to lead me home?
when my heart leads, my mind lags, dancing
and processing what it has learned.
when my mind leads, i am all too aware
and this inextricable core of my being
closes doors my heart has always been open to.

each day i forget what i remember

and remember what i forget.
except that to love
and to be enveloped
in joy isn't who i used to be
it's who i am.
still, today -
the world spins on its axis
searching for paths
that are divine
i must simply be willing
to consistently choose
mine.

what God said to the beautiful, broken man

here go a whole heart.
here go a bright pink bicycle
with butterflies.

here go a crooked spine.

here go a wide truth.
here go a soil thick with
mama love

here go a soulflower
here go a dragonfly

here go an 8th light
here go a sweet magic
here go a surrender

here go a holy spirit
here go metal clouds
here go a voice
here go a good cry

here go shame

here go forgiveness

here go a star galaxy
here go a word
here go a book

here go a harmony
here go a big world
here go fresh takes

here go your freedom

here go a beautiful
night's rest for you

here go a lean in so close
here go a power so deep
it is a vine
here go a terebinth
here go a daisy
here go a dandelion
blown back
catching the wind

the parable of the flower

10

don't you worry
whether you'll
get enough
light from the sun?

no. my only job
is to bloom.

mad enough to live

and of course
my love
i have the right to be mad
but then where would this leave us?

you were born with a voice
i had to dig up mine
you were born with belonging
i had to earn mine
therefore, dear one...
i must ride the winding waves of resistance
resilience be my guiding light
a million ancestors on my back
and we go on

because the truth is we are all
one prayer away from losing it
and some of us are meant to be gold
purified by fire

i am stardust
i am mirth and clay
i am the valley and the mountaintop
we were made to survive

we were made to thrive

i am love washed over by the tide
the soil in my lungs
something awful

breathing life into
river and starved rock
with my left hand to my right heart
my open belly and closed throat
my scabbed back and broken spirit

i come alive inside of death
and i turn it into something
yearned for, something
unwieldy and holy

the fault in our mars

13

too close to our hearts we hold
family secrets
covenants we make across bloodlines
convenient trade-offs
honesty and character trapped inside
dilapidated buildings
stripped
pressed down
shaken together
new and used pipelines
this work overflows like
water in the Dakota access
brick and mortar remorse
survival is how
we made it.

we are the dust and the sky
which rumbles under the earth

we make it work.
work makes us.
shapes us.
mothers are like Gods

with generational privilege
we make the work
we make the prayers
the work is in the prayers we make.

prayers are like promises
promises are the work made whole
we make the prayers, we keep
God as the Promise
and this is the truest nature
of a woman's work

from ferguson to floyd

i see us.
and we are breaking.
i see fire and rage
and history is becoming ashes
and we are breaking.

i see us.
and we are tired
smoke bombs and tear gas
cries of injustice amidst screams of pains
and we are tired and breaking

i see us
and we are afraid
if we miss this chance
we may never be heard again
they might take us by the throats
and rip out our vocal chords with bare hands
and say they followed the law

i see us
and we have given up
we are broken
broken down

broken into
broken open
we are breaking
we are wounded
we are everything
we are nothing
and so we fight
we fight to stay afloat
the way hope does.

i see us.

5.8.17 (three days before)

dig up the roots
stand firmly
the core of the earth
will hold you
let spirit be your guide
there are no muses here
only the harsh realities
of broken soil

open flesh
wounds that seek release
refuge for a heart
weak
crumble the dirt inside you
your moist hands
stand
for truth
healing is a garden
we will never
master

roots and wings

and finally
when i cease to
hold my breath
i begin with the moon;
nowhere to be found

my fears drowned
inside the rolling thunder
my throat swelled
my brain ripe
with new ideas
the taste of
newfound freedom
on my cracked lips
i drool
spilled upon
my left thigh

wet with possibility
and promise

5.11.17 (the day you left)

there is no distance
in the spirit

prayers from a manhattan hotel
prayers from glenview
prayers from alabama
prayers from chicago
prayers from lisle

we planted seeds
snatched up the deep roots
truth is
it was too late
his spirit had crossed over

the call came
his name etched
deep in my bones
broke me wide open
left me in despair
that would take years
to repair

it wasn't fair

it wasn't fate
we'd just spoken
and i hate
i couldn't save you

the guilt ate me alive

you didn't survive
long enough
to see the next sunrise
and while silent cries
aren't heard they are felt
you dealt with
a hopelessness
i'll never know

so until we meet again
i will honor you with my pen
i'll construct a rainbow
to brighten the shadows
of my wearied soul

to hold you close
to be whole again

5th chakra

there are a million ways to listen;
yet only one way to be heard -
speak.

let words be a life raft
floating infinitely
into blissful song.

let the cords of your throat
be a vocal thread
to connect, to make space
to build community.

let the movement
of your tongue be a rhythm
a sacred soul chant
a ritual
a new prayer
a revelation.

let the purpose
of each syllable
spilling from your lips
be to elevate hope

and eradicate the pain
of a forced silence.

let this manifesto
become a spell broken
a wish fulfilled
a new way of claiming
liberation.

let this bold instrument
be a conscious choice
birthed from intent
amplified by the promise

that the universe has opened
just by hearing
your "you-ness"
cracked open.

catch and release

it's funny how little it takes to
get me honest.

i find strength in my convictions;
no matter how twisted –
when i'm with you.

ours is the kind of strength
where we see each other
out the corner of our eyes
as we walk through doors
or past people and pictures on walls
apparently unintended for us

and you're holding my hand
and i'm holding yours

the funny thing about the irony of gratitude –
it seems to resist the gravity of burdens
blasting out millions of the tiniest particles of hope

thank you for asking and
truly wanting it –
it being

Truth.

my truth.

and you're holding my hand
and i'm holding yours
maybe we're smiling
maybe we're humming
maybe we're saying, "fuck it".

perhaps it's the way you summon us
up mountains of exposure,
standing tall at the peak
with little room for falling,
yet always ready to

catch
and
release

us.

infinite portals

what were you thinking
as the wind swept between
your tall green blades?

me, i was thinking
of life and death
the space that exists in
the middle

who were we before this
reality crushed us
back to check on
what thrives in us
when all around us
is quiet thorns

staffed with creative urge
and surrender to the mystery
our hearts beat in melancholic
holy and steady wanting

this is the beginning
of what came before the end
we can win over trust

with each step

forgive yourselves my loves
for darkness isn't quite what
it used to be
now we are infinite portals and embers
ablaze with transparency

i didn't know what you felt -
yet the questions alone seem to
answer themselves

this is grace

some days a portal
seems to open just for me
i step through it like marks
in a painting

dreading the dry nature
of my harsh reality
trauma rains on us right now

etched in my scar is a sliver of hope
my hands reach for my grandma
her coffin blooming before me

a life written across the
delicate edges of her handkerchief
after all she was a peppermint-giving
old negro spiritual singing gem
whose body now rests
in the same hands that hold me.

i am alive
and my aliveness is all i owe anyone
who continues to knock

pressed against the hard edges
of these soft tissues

spasms release into air
mixed with snow and sunshine

all we ever are
is energy.

great migration

i imagine heaven to be a colorful place
where I can open up my heart
to perpetual splendor

spinning circles
around sandcastles
in sunsets
of violet and magenta
illuminating
a once clouded
vision

there's no need
for imagination
here

where
the illustrious
sensations
of a joy so turbulent
it unearths and erupts
you
into a
million little

pieces of
vibrant laughter

even the butterflies
are high on this
grandiose state
of euphoric notion

Love is the CEO here
yet she floats by unnoticed
because
no one wants to be in charge
when Spirit
leads the march
towards expansion

its a space
of deep connection
of soul chants
and rhythmic truth
enhancing the sacred
dance you do

when you
no longer
need
a lover

or a human embrace

moment to moment
everything shifts
and since catastrophe
no longer exists

we make
infinite wishlists
for those to come

we pray they
are prepared to party
to part ways with what was
and be grounded here

we lend them
our vision and weave
with precision
whatever is needed
for this transition

after all it is
our decision

so while i've

endured hell

i allow heaven
to be a home inside me

rebirth

rise and shine
my love; greet the dawn
that awaits you.

rise and shine
my love; your tears
have cultivated
fresh soil.

rise and shine
my love; step in
to this new earth.

rise and shine
my love; give birth
to all inside you.

rise and shine
my love; sow prayer
where there is seed.

rise and shine
dear heart—

for you need only
to give voice
to what is calling you
forth...

ignited

the drip-drop of gas kissed by a match
burnt rubber tires screeching to a halt
in time with no tune
rising
walking barefoot on nails and concrete reality
back to where it all started
the brick storehouse of my emotions
encased in sweaty-palmed memories
nostrils flared
pulse racing
a fire blazes inside me
rising
heartbeat races beyond my thoughts
no childhood
all I got is broken pieces
my blood is boiling
as I am tired of being skipped over and
overlooked like
iced over membranes laced with tiny grains of salt
thoughts gurgling over into spit
a volcanic explosion of words exposes me
agony gushing out
and though the walls come tumbling down

i am reduced to a spill of rage
rising.

broken open

As the strong one
the one hurting hearts look to, to be the light
my fight feeling like
this ain't right
but i might give up
zero fucks to give
losing the will to live
a good day consists
of missed opportunities
for self care
not fair
that i
so easily share
love with the masses
spiritually bypassing
my own needs
breathing through
constant anxiety
hiding from society
cause deep inside me
lies a place that so
desperately needs
to be held
heard

gifted encouraging words
the way i tend to without trying
i think i'm dying
no, not suicide
it's just
my soul is tied
and
i have nothing
left to give
not even to my
own self
my mental health
been taking L's
for the last few years
and my tears spill out
over commercials
and acts of kindness
my mindfulness
is on vacation
this nation of liberty
has left the god in me
hard to see
so i humbly
ask
that if you could
pray for me
it'd be most appreciated

too complicated
to explain
too many words
to describe
what life
has done to me
my bipolar reality
a new normalcy
my currency is energy
but you can't give
what you don't get
my chemical imbalance
has been a challenge
a dance between
balancing the day to day
or always wanting to
run away
and damn this poem
is longer than
i expected it to be
but to reject this part of me
would be a grave mistake
so i take my time
and let it finish
so as not to diminish
my spirit
and if you hear it

let it be known
that my microphone
is back on
i'm waging war
with my pen again
and also
i could really
use a friend
right
now

whispers in the river

i channel the stillness like a river
where bourbon skies fade into night,
sipping on silence, I search for the sage
whose wisdom drifts just out of sight.

a hymn hums soft beneath the trees,
a song woven in the wind's sweet chant,
meditation carries the unseen threads
of holy dreams where I dare to plant.

in the divine quiet, I find my place,
a sanctuary where the wild things roam,
where the unseen flows through everything,
and I call this holy river my home.

www.ingramcontent.com/pod-product-compliance
Lightning Source LLC
LaVergne TN
LVHW050945200726
843508LV00011B/2448